50 Flavors of the Far East
Recipes for Home

By: Kelly Johnson

Table of Contents

- Thai Green Curry
- Korean Bibimbap
- Japanese Ramen
- Vietnamese Pho
- Chinese Dumplings
- Thai Pad Thai
- Korean BBQ Beef
- Japanese Sushi Rolls
- Vietnamese Banh Mi
- Chinese Kung Pao Chicken
- Thai Tom Yum Soup
- Japanese Teriyaki Chicken
- Korean Kimchi Fried Rice
- Vietnamese Spring Rolls
- Chinese Sweet and Sour Pork
- Thai Mango Sticky Rice
- Japanese Tempura
- Korean Spicy Chicken Wings
- Vietnamese Lemongrass Pork
- Chinese Hot and Sour Soup
- Thai Red Curry Noodles
- Japanese Miso Soup
- Korean Beef Bulgogi
- Vietnamese Grilled Pork Chops
- Chinese Chow Mein
- Thai Cashew Chicken
- Japanese Udon Noodles
- Korean Spicy Tofu Soup
- Vietnamese Beef Salad
- Chinese Egg Drop Soup
- Thai Pineapple Fried Rice
- Japanese Yakitori Skewers
- Korean Chicken Katsu
- Vietnamese Pho Ga (Chicken Pho)
- Chinese General Tso's Chicken

- Thai Green Papaya Salad
- Japanese Shabu-Shabu
- Korean Japchae (Stir-Fried Noodles)
- Vietnamese Caramelized Fish
- Chinese Lemon Chicken
- Thai Red Curry with Duck
- Japanese Tonkatsu
- Korean Spicy Pork Belly
- Vietnamese Bun Cha
- Chinese Szechuan Eggplant
- Thai Lemongrass Chicken
- Japanese Okonomiyaki
- Korean Steamed Egg
- Vietnamese Egg Coffee
- Chinese Peking Duck

Thai Green Curry

Ingredients:

- 1 lb chicken breasts, sliced
- 2 tbsp green curry paste
- 1 can (14 oz) coconut milk
- 1 cup chicken broth
- 1 bell pepper, sliced
- 1 zucchini, sliced
- 1 cup bamboo shoots, drained
- 2 tbsp fish sauce
- 1 tbsp brown sugar
- Fresh basil leaves for garnish
- Steamed jasmine rice for serving

Instructions:

1. **Cook Chicken:** In a large skillet, cook chicken over medium heat until browned.
2. **Add Curry Paste:** Stir in green curry paste and cook for 1 minute.
3. **Add Liquids:** Pour in coconut milk and chicken broth. Bring to a simmer.
4. **Add Vegetables:** Stir in bell pepper, zucchini, and bamboo shoots. Cook until vegetables are tender.
5. **Season:** Stir in fish sauce and brown sugar. Adjust seasoning if necessary.
6. **Serve:** Garnish with fresh basil leaves and serve over jasmine rice.

Korean Bibimbap

Ingredients:

- 2 cups cooked rice
- 1 cup spinach, sautéed
- 1 cup bean sprouts, blanched
- 1 cup julienned carrots
- 1 cup shiitake mushrooms, sautéed
- 1/2 lb ground beef, cooked with Korean seasoning
- 2 eggs
- 2 tbsp gochujang (Korean red chili paste)
- Sesame oil for drizzling
- Sesame seeds for garnish
- Sliced green onions for garnish

Instructions:

1. **Prepare Vegetables:** Sauté spinach, bean sprouts, carrots, and mushrooms separately until cooked.
2. **Cook Beef:** Cook ground beef with Korean seasoning (soy sauce, sugar, sesame oil, and garlic).
3. **Fry Eggs:** In a separate pan, fry eggs sunny-side up.
4. **Assemble Bibimbap:** In bowls, place a portion of rice. Arrange vegetables and beef on top.
5. **Add Toppings:** Place a fried egg in the center, drizzle with sesame oil, and garnish with sesame seeds and green onions.
6. **Serve:** Serve with gochujang on the side.

Japanese Ramen

Ingredients:

- 4 cups chicken or pork broth
- 2 packs ramen noodles
- 1 tbsp miso paste
- 2 cloves garlic, minced
- 1 tbsp soy sauce
- 1 tbsp sesame oil
- 1 cup sliced mushrooms
- 1 cup baby spinach
- 2 green onions, sliced
- 2 soft-boiled eggs
- Sliced cooked pork or chicken for topping

Instructions:

1. **Prepare Broth:** In a pot, heat sesame oil and sauté garlic until fragrant. Stir in miso paste, then add broth.
2. **Cook Noodles:** Add ramen noodles and cook according to package instructions.
3. **Add Vegetables:** Stir in mushrooms and cook until tender. Add spinach and cook until wilted.
4. **Season:** Stir in soy sauce and adjust seasoning if needed.
5. **Serve:** Divide noodles into bowls. Ladle broth and vegetables over noodles. Top with sliced pork or chicken, soft-boiled eggs, and green onions.

Vietnamese Pho

Ingredients:

- 4 cups beef broth
- 1 onion, halved
- 1 piece ginger, sliced
- 2 cloves garlic, minced
- 1 tbsp fish sauce
- 1 tbsp soy sauce
- 1 cinnamon stick
- 2 star anise
- 1 lb beef sirloin, thinly sliced
- Rice noodles, cooked according to package instructions
- Fresh basil leaves
- Bean sprouts
- Lime wedges
- Sliced jalapeños

Instructions:

1. **Prepare Broth:** In a large pot, simmer beef broth with onion, ginger, garlic, fish sauce, soy sauce, cinnamon stick, and star anise for 30 minutes.
2. **Strain Broth:** Remove solids and strain the broth.
3. **Cook Beef:** Thinly slice beef and briefly cook in the hot broth until just done.
4. **Assemble Pho:** Place cooked noodles in bowls. Ladle hot broth over the noodles and beef.
5. **Garnish:** Serve with fresh basil, bean sprouts, lime wedges, and sliced jalapeños.

Chinese Dumplings

Ingredients:

- 1/2 lb ground pork
- 1/2 cup finely chopped cabbage
- 1/4 cup finely chopped green onions
- 1 tbsp soy sauce
- 1 tbsp sesame oil
- 1 tbsp minced ginger
- 1 tbsp minced garlic
- Dumpling wrappers
- Soy sauce for dipping

Instructions:

1. **Prepare Filling:** In a bowl, mix ground pork, cabbage, green onions, soy sauce, sesame oil, ginger, and garlic.
2. **Fill Dumplings:** Place a small amount of filling in the center of each dumpling wrapper. Fold and seal the edges.
3. **Cook Dumplings:** Steam dumplings for 15 minutes or pan-fry until golden and cooked through.
4. **Serve:** Serve with soy sauce for dipping.

Thai Pad Thai

Ingredients:

- 8 oz rice noodles
- 2 tbsp vegetable oil
- 1 cup cooked shrimp or chicken
- 2 eggs, lightly beaten
- 1 cup bean sprouts
- 1/4 cup chopped peanuts
- 2 green onions, sliced
- 1/4 cup tamarind paste
- 3 tbsp fish sauce
- 2 tbsp sugar
- Lime wedges for serving

Instructions:

1. **Cook Noodles:** Cook rice noodles according to package instructions. Drain and set aside.
2. **Cook Protein:** In a large pan, heat vegetable oil. Add shrimp or chicken and cook until done. Remove and set aside.
3. **Scramble Eggs:** In the same pan, add beaten eggs and scramble until cooked.
4. **Combine Ingredients:** Add cooked noodles, bean sprouts, peanuts, green onions, tamarind paste, fish sauce, and sugar. Toss to combine and heat through.
5. **Serve:** Serve with lime wedges.

Korean BBQ Beef

Ingredients:

- 1 lb beef ribeye, thinly sliced
- 1/4 cup soy sauce
- 2 tbsp sesame oil
- 2 tbsp brown sugar
- 2 cloves garlic, minced
- 1 tbsp grated ginger
- 2 green onions, sliced
- 1 tbsp sesame seeds
- Cooked rice for serving

Instructions:

1. **Marinate Beef:** In a bowl, combine soy sauce, sesame oil, brown sugar, garlic, and ginger. Add beef and marinate for at least 30 minutes.
2. **Cook Beef:** In a skillet or grill pan, cook marinated beef over medium-high heat until browned and cooked through.
3. **Serve:** Garnish with green onions and sesame seeds. Serve with cooked rice.

Japanese Sushi Rolls

Ingredients:

- 2 cups sushi rice, cooked
- 1/4 cup rice vinegar
- 1 tbsp sugar
- 1/2 tsp salt
- Nori (seaweed) sheets
- Fillings (e.g., cucumber, avocado, cooked crab or fish)
- Soy sauce for dipping
- Pickled ginger and wasabi for serving

Instructions:

1. **Prepare Rice:** In a bowl, mix rice vinegar, sugar, and salt. Stir into cooked rice and let cool slightly.
2. **Assemble Rolls:** Place a nori sheet on a bamboo sushi mat. Spread a thin layer of rice over nori, leaving a border at the top edge. Arrange fillings on top of rice.
3. **Roll Sushi:** Using the mat, roll the sushi tightly, pressing gently.
4. **Cut Rolls:** Slice rolls into bite-sized pieces.
5. **Serve:** Serve with soy sauce, pickled ginger, and wasabi.

Vietnamese Banh Mi

Ingredients:

- 1 baguette
- 1/2 lb pork loin, thinly sliced
- 1/4 cup hoisin sauce
- 2 tbsp soy sauce
- 1 tbsp sugar
- 1 tbsp vegetable oil
- 1/2 cup pickled carrots and daikon (or store-bought)
- 1 cucumber, sliced
- Fresh cilantro
- Sliced jalapeños
- Mayonnaise

Instructions:

1. **Marinate Pork:** Combine hoisin sauce, soy sauce, sugar, and vegetable oil. Marinate pork slices for at least 30 minutes.
2. **Cook Pork:** Grill or pan-fry pork slices until cooked through.
3. **Assemble Banh Mi:** Slice baguette and spread a layer of mayonnaise on one side. Layer with pork, pickled carrots and daikon, cucumber, cilantro, and jalapeños.
4. **Serve:** Serve immediately or wrap for later.

Chinese Kung Pao Chicken

Ingredients:

- 1 lb chicken breasts, diced
- 2 tbsp soy sauce
- 2 tbsp rice vinegar
- 2 tbsp hoisin sauce
- 1 tbsp cornstarch
- 1/4 cup vegetable oil
- 1/2 cup roasted peanuts
- 1 bell pepper, chopped
- 1 onion, chopped
- 3 cloves garlic, minced
- 1 tbsp ginger, minced
- 2 tbsp sugar
- 1/4 cup chicken broth
- 1/4 tsp red pepper flakes (optional)
- 2 green onions, sliced

Instructions:

1. **Prepare Sauce:** In a bowl, mix soy sauce, rice vinegar, hoisin sauce, and cornstarch.
2. **Cook Chicken:** Heat oil in a large skillet over medium-high heat. Cook chicken until browned and cooked through. Remove and set aside.
3. **Sauté Vegetables:** In the same skillet, add bell pepper, onion, garlic, and ginger. Cook until vegetables are tender.
4. **Combine:** Return chicken to the skillet. Add sauce, sugar, chicken broth, and red pepper flakes. Stir well and cook until sauce thickens.
5. **Serve:** Garnish with peanuts and green onions. Serve over rice.

Thai Tom Yum Soup

Ingredients:

- 4 cups chicken or vegetable broth
- 1 stalk lemongrass, sliced
- 3-4 kaffir lime leaves
- 3 slices galangal (or ginger)
- 1 cup mushrooms, sliced
- 1 cup shrimp, peeled and deveined
- 2-3 Thai bird chilies, smashed
- 2 tbsp fish sauce
- 1 tbsp lime juice
- 1 tsp sugar
- Fresh cilantro for garnish

Instructions:

1. **Prepare Broth:** In a pot, bring broth to a boil. Add lemongrass, kaffir lime leaves, and galangal. Simmer for 10 minutes.
2. **Add Ingredients:** Stir in mushrooms and cook until tender. Add shrimp and cook until pink.
3. **Season:** Add bird chilies, fish sauce, lime juice, and sugar. Adjust seasoning to taste.
4. **Serve:** Garnish with fresh cilantro and serve hot.

Japanese Teriyaki Chicken

Ingredients:

- 4 boneless, skinless chicken thighs
- 1/4 cup soy sauce
- 1/4 cup mirin (sweet rice wine)
- 2 tbsp sake (optional)
- 2 tbsp sugar
- 1 tbsp vegetable oil
- Sesame seeds for garnish
- Sliced green onions for garnish

Instructions:

1. **Prepare Sauce:** In a bowl, mix soy sauce, mirin, sake, and sugar.
2. **Cook Chicken:** Heat oil in a skillet over medium heat. Cook chicken thighs until browned and cooked through.
3. **Add Sauce:** Pour teriyaki sauce over chicken and simmer until sauce thickens and coats the chicken.
4. **Serve:** Garnish with sesame seeds and green onions. Serve with rice.

Korean Kimchi Fried Rice

Ingredients:

- 2 cups cooked rice
- 1 cup kimchi, chopped
- 1/2 cup kimchi juice
- 1/2 lb ground pork
- 2 cloves garlic, minced
- 2 green onions, chopped
- 2 eggs, lightly beaten
- 2 tbsp soy sauce
- 1 tbsp sesame oil
- Sesame seeds for garnish

Instructions:

1. **Cook Pork:** In a large skillet, heat sesame oil and cook ground pork until browned.
2. **Add Kimchi:** Stir in kimchi and kimchi juice. Cook for 2-3 minutes.
3. **Add Rice:** Add rice and soy sauce, stirring well to combine. Cook until heated through.
4. **Add Eggs:** Push rice to one side of the skillet and scramble eggs on the other side. Mix eggs into rice.
5. **Serve:** Garnish with green onions and sesame seeds.

Vietnamese Spring Rolls

Ingredients:

- 12 rice paper wrappers
- 1 cup cooked shrimp, sliced
- 1 cup lettuce leaves
- 1 cup rice vermicelli noodles, cooked
- 1/2 cup shredded carrots
- 1/2 cup fresh mint leaves
- 1/2 cup fresh cilantro leaves
- Peanut dipping sauce or hoisin sauce

Instructions:

1. **Prepare Fillings:** Arrange lettuce, vermicelli noodles, carrots, mint, cilantro, and shrimp in a line on a plate.
2. **Soften Wrappers:** Dip rice paper wrappers in warm water until softened, then lay flat on a clean surface.
3. **Assemble Rolls:** Place a small amount of each filling in the center of the wrapper. Fold sides and roll tightly.
4. **Serve:** Serve with peanut or hoisin dipping sauce.

Chinese Sweet and Sour Pork

Ingredients:

- 1 lb pork tenderloin, cut into bite-sized pieces
- 1/2 cup cornstarch
- 2 tbsp vegetable oil
- 1 bell pepper, chopped
- 1 onion, chopped
- 1 cup pineapple chunks
- 1/2 cup sweet and sour sauce
- 2 tbsp soy sauce
- 1 tbsp rice vinegar

Instructions:

1. **Coat Pork:** Toss pork pieces in cornstarch to coat.
2. **Fry Pork:** Heat oil in a large skillet or wok. Fry pork in batches until golden and cooked through. Remove and set aside.
3. **Cook Vegetables:** In the same skillet, stir-fry bell pepper and onion until tender.
4. **Add Sauce:** Stir in pineapple chunks, sweet and sour sauce, soy sauce, and rice vinegar. Cook until heated through.
5. **Combine:** Return pork to the skillet and toss to coat in sauce.
6. **Serve:** Serve hot over rice.

Thai Mango Sticky Rice

Ingredients:

- 1 cup glutinous rice
- 1 1/2 cups coconut milk
- 1/2 cup sugar
- 1/4 tsp salt
- 2 ripe mangoes, peeled and sliced
- Sesame seeds or toasted coconut for garnish

Instructions:

1. **Cook Rice:** Rinse rice until water runs clear. Cook rice according to package instructions or steam for about 30 minutes.
2. **Prepare Coconut Sauce:** In a saucepan, heat coconut milk, sugar, and salt until sugar is dissolved.
3. **Combine:** Stir 1 cup of coconut sauce into cooked rice. Let rice absorb the sauce and cool slightly.
4. **Serve:** Serve rice with mango slices. Garnish with sesame seeds or toasted coconut.

Japanese Tempura

Ingredients:

- 1 cup all-purpose flour
- 1/2 cup cornstarch
- 1 egg, lightly beaten
- 1 cup cold water
- 12 large shrimp, peeled and deveined
- 1 cup vegetables (e.g., sweet potato, zucchini, bell pepper), sliced
- Vegetable oil for frying
- Tempura dipping sauce (store-bought or homemade)

Instructions:

1. **Prepare Batter:** In a bowl, mix flour and cornstarch. Add beaten egg and cold water, stirring gently until just combined. The batter should be lumpy.
2. **Heat Oil:** Heat oil in a deep fryer or large pot to 350°F (175°C).
3. **Coat and Fry:** Dip shrimp and vegetables in the batter, allowing excess to drip off. Fry in batches until golden and crispy, about 2-3 minutes.
4. **Drain and Serve:** Remove with a slotted spoon and drain on paper towels. Serve with tempura dipping sauce.

Korean Spicy Chicken Wings

Ingredients:

- 2 lbs chicken wings
- 1/4 cup soy sauce
- 1/4 cup gochujang (Korean chili paste)
- 2 tbsp honey
- 2 tbsp rice vinegar
- 3 cloves garlic, minced
- 1 tbsp ginger, minced
- 1 tbsp sesame oil
- Sesame seeds for garnish
- Sliced green onions for garnish

Instructions:

1. **Prepare Marinade:** In a bowl, mix soy sauce, gochujang, honey, rice vinegar, garlic, ginger, and sesame oil.
2. **Marinate Wings:** Toss chicken wings in the marinade and refrigerate for at least 1 hour.
3. **Cook Wings:** Preheat oven to 400°F (200°C). Arrange wings on a baking sheet and bake for 30-35 minutes, turning halfway through.
4. **Garnish and Serve:** Garnish with sesame seeds and green onions. Serve hot.

Vietnamese Lemongrass Pork

Ingredients:

- 1 lb pork shoulder, thinly sliced
- 2 tbsp lemongrass, finely chopped
- 3 cloves garlic, minced
- 2 tbsp fish sauce
- 1 tbsp soy sauce
- 1 tbsp sugar
- 1 tbsp vegetable oil
- Fresh cilantro for garnish

Instructions:

1. **Prepare Marinade:** In a bowl, mix lemongrass, garlic, fish sauce, soy sauce, and sugar.
2. **Marinate Pork:** Toss pork slices in the marinade and let sit for at least 30 minutes.
3. **Cook Pork:** Heat oil in a skillet over medium-high heat. Cook pork until browned and cooked through, about 5-7 minutes.
4. **Serve:** Garnish with fresh cilantro. Serve with rice.

Chinese Hot and Sour Soup

Ingredients:

- 4 cups chicken or vegetable broth
- 1 cup mushrooms, sliced
- 1/2 cup tofu, cubed
- 1/4 cup soy sauce
- 2 tbsp rice vinegar
- 1 tbsp cornstarch mixed with 2 tbsp water
- 1 tsp white pepper
- 1/2 tsp sesame oil
- 1 egg, lightly beaten
- Sliced green onions for garnish
- Fresh cilantro for garnish

Instructions:

1. **Prepare Soup Base:** In a pot, bring broth to a boil. Add mushrooms and tofu, cooking until mushrooms are tender.
2. **Add Seasonings:** Stir in soy sauce, rice vinegar, and white pepper.
3. **Thicken Soup:** Add cornstarch mixture, stirring until soup thickens.
4. **Add Egg:** Slowly drizzle in beaten egg while stirring to create egg ribbons.
5. **Serve:** Garnish with green onions and cilantro. Serve hot.

Thai Red Curry Noodles

Ingredients:

- 8 oz rice noodles
- 1 tbsp vegetable oil
- 1 tbsp red curry paste
- 1 can (13.5 oz) coconut milk
- 1 tbsp fish sauce
- 1 tbsp brown sugar
- 1 cup mixed vegetables (e.g., bell peppers, carrots, snap peas)
- 1/2 cup basil leaves
- Lime wedges for serving

Instructions:

1. **Cook Noodles:** Cook rice noodles according to package instructions. Drain and set aside.
2. **Prepare Sauce:** In a large pan, heat oil and sauté red curry paste until fragrant. Add coconut milk, fish sauce, and brown sugar, stirring to combine.
3. **Add Vegetables:** Stir in mixed vegetables and cook until tender.
4. **Combine:** Add cooked noodles and toss to coat in the curry sauce.
5. **Serve:** Garnish with basil leaves and serve with lime wedges.

Japanese Miso Soup

Ingredients:

- 4 cups dashi broth (or chicken/vegetable broth)
- 1/4 cup miso paste
- 1/2 cup tofu, cubed
- 1/4 cup sliced green onions
- 1/4 cup wakame seaweed (optional)

Instructions:

1. **Heat Broth:** In a pot, heat dashi broth to a simmer.
2. **Prepare Miso:** Dissolve miso paste in a small amount of warm broth, then stir back into the pot.
3. **Add Tofu and Seaweed:** Add tofu and wakame (if using) to the soup and heat through.
4. **Serve:** Garnish with green onions. Serve hot.

Korean Beef Bulgogi

Ingredients:

- 1 lb beef sirloin, thinly sliced
- 1/4 cup soy sauce
- 2 tbsp sugar
- 2 tbsp sesame oil
- 3 cloves garlic, minced
- 1 tbsp ginger, minced
- 1/4 cup sliced green onions
- 1 tbsp sesame seeds

Instructions:

1. **Prepare Marinade:** In a bowl, mix soy sauce, sugar, sesame oil, garlic, and ginger.
2. **Marinate Beef:** Toss beef slices in the marinade and refrigerate for at least 1 hour.
3. **Cook Beef:** Heat a skillet over medium-high heat. Cook beef until browned and cooked through.
4. **Serve:** Garnish with green onions and sesame seeds. Serve with rice.

Vietnamese Grilled Pork Chops

Ingredients:

- 4 pork chops
- 1/4 cup fish sauce
- 2 tbsp sugar
- 1 tbsp soy sauce
- 3 cloves garlic, minced
- 1 tbsp lemongrass, finely chopped
- 1 tbsp vegetable oil

Instructions:

1. **Prepare Marinade:** In a bowl, mix fish sauce, sugar, soy sauce, garlic, lemongrass, and oil.
2. **Marinate Pork:** Toss pork chops in the marinade and let sit for at least 1 hour.
3. **Grill Pork:** Preheat grill to medium-high heat. Grill pork chops until cooked through and grill marks appear, about 4-5 minutes per side.
4. **Serve:** Serve with rice or a side salad.

Chinese Chow Mein

Ingredients:

- 8 oz chow mein noodles
- 2 tbsp vegetable oil
- 1 cup sliced chicken breast or beef
- 1 cup broccoli florets
- 1 cup sliced bell peppers
- 1 cup sliced carrots
- 3 cloves garlic, minced
- 1 tbsp soy sauce
- 2 tbsp oyster sauce
- 1 tbsp hoisin sauce
- 1/2 tsp sesame oil
- Sliced green onions for garnish

Instructions:

1. **Cook Noodles:** Cook chow mein noodles according to package instructions. Drain and set aside.
2. **Stir-Fry Meat:** Heat vegetable oil in a large skillet or wok over medium-high heat. Add sliced meat and cook until browned.
3. **Add Vegetables:** Add garlic and vegetables to the skillet. Stir-fry until vegetables are tender-crisp.
4. **Combine Noodles and Sauce:** Add cooked noodles, soy sauce, oyster sauce, hoisin sauce, and sesame oil to the skillet. Toss everything together until well coated and heated through.
5. **Serve:** Garnish with sliced green onions. Serve hot.

Thai Cashew Chicken

Ingredients:

- 1 lb chicken breast, cut into bite-sized pieces
- 2 tbsp vegetable oil
- 1/2 cup cashews
- 1 cup sliced bell peppers
- 1 cup sliced onions
- 1 cup snap peas
- 3 cloves garlic, minced
- 1 tbsp ginger, minced
- 3 tbsp soy sauce
- 2 tbsp fish sauce
- 1 tbsp brown sugar
- 1 tbsp lime juice
- Fresh cilantro for garnish

Instructions:

1. **Cook Chicken:** Heat oil in a skillet over medium-high heat. Add chicken and cook until no longer pink.
2. **Add Vegetables:** Add garlic, ginger, bell peppers, onions, and snap peas to the skillet. Stir-fry until vegetables are tender.
3. **Prepare Sauce:** In a small bowl, mix soy sauce, fish sauce, brown sugar, and lime juice. Add to the skillet and toss to coat.
4. **Add Cashews:** Stir in cashews and cook for an additional 2 minutes.
5. **Serve:** Garnish with fresh cilantro. Serve with rice.

Japanese Udon Noodles

Ingredients:

- 8 oz udon noodles
- 2 tbsp vegetable oil
- 1 cup sliced mushrooms
- 1 cup sliced bok choy
- 1/2 cup sliced carrots
- 2 cloves garlic, minced
- 1 tbsp soy sauce
- 1 tbsp mirin
- 2 tbsp miso paste
- 2 cups vegetable or chicken broth
- Sliced green onions for garnish

Instructions:

1. **Cook Noodles:** Cook udon noodles according to package instructions. Drain and set aside.
2. **Prepare Broth:** In a pot, heat oil and sauté garlic until fragrant. Add mushrooms, bok choy, and carrots. Stir-fry for 3-4 minutes.
3. **Add Broth and Miso:** Add broth and miso paste to the pot. Stir until miso is dissolved and the mixture comes to a simmer.
4. **Combine Noodles:** Add cooked udon noodles to the pot and heat through.
5. **Serve:** Garnish with sliced green onions. Serve hot.

Korean Spicy Tofu Soup

Ingredients:

- 1 block firm tofu, cubed
- 1 tbsp vegetable oil
- 1 cup sliced mushrooms
- 1 cup sliced kimchi
- 2 cups vegetable broth
- 2 tbsp gochujang (Korean chili paste)
- 2 cloves garlic, minced
- 1 tbsp soy sauce
- 1 tsp sesame oil
- Green onions for garnish

Instructions:

1. **Prepare Soup Base:** Heat oil in a pot over medium heat. Sauté garlic until fragrant. Add mushrooms and kimchi, cooking for 3-4 minutes.
2. **Add Broth and Spice:** Add vegetable broth and gochujang to the pot. Stir until gochujang is fully incorporated.
3. **Add Tofu:** Gently add tofu cubes to the soup and simmer for 5-7 minutes.
4. **Finish and Serve:** Stir in sesame oil. Garnish with green onions. Serve hot.

Vietnamese Beef Salad

Ingredients:

- 1 lb beef sirloin, thinly sliced
- 4 cups mixed salad greens
- 1 cup shredded carrots
- 1/2 cup sliced cucumber
- 1/2 cup cherry tomatoes, halved
- 1/4 cup fresh mint leaves
- 1/4 cup fresh cilantro leaves
- 3 tbsp fish sauce
- 2 tbsp lime juice
- 1 tbsp sugar
- 1 tbsp vegetable oil

Instructions:

1. **Cook Beef:** Heat oil in a skillet over high heat. Cook beef slices until browned and cooked to your liking.
2. **Prepare Dressing:** In a small bowl, mix fish sauce, lime juice, and sugar until sugar dissolves.
3. **Assemble Salad:** In a large bowl, toss salad greens, carrots, cucumber, tomatoes, mint, and cilantro.
4. **Combine and Serve:** Add cooked beef to the salad, drizzle with dressing, and toss to combine. Serve immediately.

Chinese Egg Drop Soup

Ingredients:

- 4 cups chicken or vegetable broth
- 2 large eggs, lightly beaten
- 1 tbsp cornstarch mixed with 2 tbsp water
- 1/4 cup sliced green onions
- 1/2 cup frozen corn kernels (optional)
- 1/2 tsp sesame oil

Instructions:

1. **Prepare Broth:** In a pot, bring broth to a simmer.
2. **Thicken Soup:** Stir in cornstarch mixture and cook until soup thickens.
3. **Add Egg:** Slowly drizzle in beaten eggs while stirring to create egg ribbons.
4. **Finish and Serve:** Stir in sesame oil and green onions. Serve hot.

Thai Pineapple Fried Rice

Ingredients:

- 2 cups cooked jasmine rice (preferably cold)
- 2 tbsp vegetable oil
- 1 cup diced pineapple
- 1/2 cup diced bell peppers
- 1/2 cup peas
- 2 cloves garlic, minced
- 2 tbsp soy sauce
- 1 tbsp fish sauce
- 1/2 tsp turmeric
- 2 eggs, lightly beaten
- Sliced green onions for garnish

Instructions:

1. **Heat Oil:** In a large skillet or wok, heat oil over medium-high heat.
2. **Stir-Fry Vegetables:** Add garlic, bell peppers, peas, and pineapple. Stir-fry for 2-3 minutes.
3. **Add Rice and Seasoning:** Add cold rice, soy sauce, fish sauce, and turmeric. Stir to combine.
4. **Add Eggs:** Push rice to one side of the skillet and pour beaten eggs into the empty space. Scramble eggs until cooked, then mix into the rice.
5. **Serve:** Garnish with green onions. Serve hot.

Japanese Yakitori Skewers

Ingredients:

- 1 lb chicken thighs, cut into bite-sized pieces
- 1/4 cup soy sauce
- 1/4 cup mirin
- 2 tbsp sugar
- 2 tbsp sake
- 1 tbsp vegetable oil
- 8-10 bamboo skewers, soaked in water

Instructions:

1. **Prepare Sauce:** In a small pot, combine soy sauce, mirin, sugar, and sake. Bring to a boil, then reduce heat and simmer for 5 minutes.
2. **Marinate Chicken:** Thread chicken pieces onto bamboo skewers. Brush with half of the sauce and marinate for at least 30 minutes.
3. **Grill Skewers:** Heat oil on a grill or in a grill pan over medium-high heat. Grill skewers, turning occasionally, until chicken is cooked through and slightly charred, about 8-10 minutes.
4. **Serve:** Brush with remaining sauce and serve hot.

Korean Chicken Katsu

Ingredients:

- 4 boneless, skinless chicken breasts
- 1 cup all-purpose flour
- 2 large eggs, beaten
- 1 cup panko breadcrumbs
- Vegetable oil for frying
- 1/2 cup tonkotsu sauce (for serving)

Instructions:

1. **Prepare Chicken:** Pound chicken breasts to an even thickness.
2. **Bread Chicken:** Dredge chicken in flour, dip in beaten eggs, and coat with panko breadcrumbs.
3. **Heat Oil:** Heat vegetable oil in a large skillet over medium heat.
4. **Fry Chicken:** Fry chicken until golden brown and cooked through, about 4-5 minutes per side.
5. **Serve:** Drain on paper towels and serve with tonkotsu sauce.

Vietnamese Pho Ga (Chicken Pho)

Ingredients:

- 1 whole chicken (about 3-4 lbs)
- 1 large onion, halved
- 2-3 slices ginger
- 4 cloves garlic, smashed
- 3-4 star anise
- 1 cinnamon stick
- 5-6 cloves
- 1 tbsp fish sauce
- 1 tbsp sugar
- 8 oz rice noodles
- Fresh basil, cilantro, lime wedges, and sliced jalapeños for serving

Instructions:

1. **Prepare Broth:** In a large pot, bring water to a boil and add the whole chicken. Simmer for about 30 minutes, then remove chicken and set aside.
2. **Flavor Broth:** Add onion, ginger, garlic, star anise, cinnamon stick, cloves, fish sauce, and sugar to the pot. Simmer for another 30 minutes.
3. **Shred Chicken:** Once cooled, shred the chicken meat and discard bones.
4. **Prepare Noodles:** Cook rice noodles according to package instructions.
5. **Assemble Pho:** Divide noodles into bowls, ladle hot broth over them, and top with shredded chicken. Garnish with basil, cilantro, lime wedges, and jalapeños.

Chinese General Tso's Chicken

Ingredients:

- 1 lb boneless chicken thighs, cut into bite-sized pieces
- 1/2 cup cornstarch
- 1/2 cup all-purpose flour
- Vegetable oil for frying
- 3 tbsp soy sauce
- 1 tbsp rice vinegar
- 1 tbsp hoisin sauce
- 1 tbsp sugar
- 1 tsp ginger, minced
- 3 cloves garlic, minced
- 1/2 cup chicken broth
- 1 tbsp sesame oil
- Sliced green onions and sesame seeds for garnish

Instructions:

1. **Bread Chicken:** Combine cornstarch and flour in a bowl. Coat chicken pieces in the mixture.
2. **Fry Chicken:** Heat oil in a large skillet over medium-high heat. Fry chicken until golden brown and cooked through, about 4-5 minutes per side.
3. **Prepare Sauce:** In a separate pan, heat sesame oil and sauté garlic and ginger until fragrant. Add soy sauce, rice vinegar, hoisin sauce, sugar, and chicken broth. Simmer until slightly thickened.
4. **Combine and Serve:** Toss fried chicken in the sauce. Garnish with green onions and sesame seeds. Serve with rice.

Thai Green Papaya Salad

Ingredients:

- 2 cups shredded green papaya
- 1 cup shredded carrots
- 1/2 cup cherry tomatoes, halved
- 1/4 cup roasted peanuts
- 2 cloves garlic, minced
- 2-3 Thai bird chilies, minced
- 2 tbsp fish sauce
- 1 tbsp lime juice
- 1 tbsp palm sugar or brown sugar

Instructions:

1. **Prepare Salad:** In a large bowl, combine shredded green papaya, carrots, and cherry tomatoes.
2. **Make Dressing:** In a small bowl, mix garlic, chilies, fish sauce, lime juice, and sugar. Stir until sugar is dissolved.
3. **Toss and Serve:** Pour dressing over the salad and toss well. Top with roasted peanuts before serving.

Japanese Shabu-Shabu

Ingredients:

- 1/2 lb thinly sliced beef (or pork)
- 4 cups dashi broth
- 2 cups mixed vegetables (e.g., bok choy, mushrooms, carrots)
- 1 cup tofu, cubed
- Soy sauce and ponzu sauce for dipping

Instructions:

1. **Heat Broth:** In a pot, bring dashi broth to a simmer.
2. **Cook Ingredients:** Cook vegetables and tofu in the simmering broth until tender.
3. **Cook Meat:** Dip slices of beef into the broth until just cooked.
4. **Serve:** Serve with soy sauce and ponzu sauce for dipping.

Korean Japchae (Stir-Fried Noodles)

Ingredients:

- 8 oz sweet potato noodles (dangmyeon)
- 2 tbsp vegetable oil
- 1 cup sliced beef
- 1 cup sliced bell peppers
- 1 cup sliced carrots
- 1 cup spinach
- 3 cloves garlic, minced
- 3 tbsp soy sauce
- 2 tbsp sugar
- 1 tbsp sesame oil
- Sesame seeds for garnish

Instructions:

1. **Cook Noodles:** Cook sweet potato noodles according to package instructions. Drain and set aside.
2. **Stir-Fry Meat:** Heat oil in a skillet over medium-high heat. Cook beef until browned.
3. **Add Vegetables:** Add garlic, bell peppers, carrots, and spinach. Stir-fry until vegetables are tender.
4. **Combine Noodles:** Add cooked noodles, soy sauce, sugar, and sesame oil to the skillet. Toss everything together until well combined and heated through.
5. **Serve:** Garnish with sesame seeds. Serve hot.

Vietnamese Caramelized Fish

Ingredients:

- 1 lb white fish fillets (e.g., tilapia)
- 1/4 cup fish sauce
- 1/4 cup sugar
- 2 cloves garlic, minced
- 1/2 cup water
- 1 tbsp vegetable oil
- 1/4 cup chopped cilantro for garnish

Instructions:

1. **Prepare Caramel Sauce:** In a pan, combine sugar and water over medium heat. Cook until sugar turns golden brown and caramelizes.
2. **Add Fish:** Add fish sauce, garlic, and vegetable oil to the caramel sauce. Stir to combine.
3. **Cook Fish:** Add fish fillets to the pan, cooking until fish is tender and cooked through.
4. **Serve:** Garnish with chopped cilantro and serve with rice.

Chinese Lemon Chicken

Ingredients:

- 1 lb boneless chicken breasts, cut into bite-sized pieces
- 1/2 cup cornstarch
- Vegetable oil for frying
- 1/2 cup lemon juice
- 1/4 cup chicken broth
- 1/4 cup sugar
- 2 tbsp soy sauce
- 1 tbsp grated ginger
- 1 tbsp soy sauce
- Sliced green onions for garnish

Instructions:

1. **Bread Chicken:** Dredge chicken pieces in cornstarch.
2. **Fry Chicken:** Heat oil in a skillet over medium-high heat. Fry chicken until golden and cooked through, about 4-5 minutes per side.
3. **Prepare Sauce:** In a separate pan, combine lemon juice, chicken broth, sugar, soy sauce, and ginger. Bring to a boil and simmer until slightly thickened.
4. **Combine and Serve:** Toss fried chicken in the lemon sauce. Garnish with green onions. Serve with rice.

Thai Red Curry with Duck

Ingredients:

- 1 lb duck breasts, sliced
- 2 tbsp red curry paste
- 1 can (13.5 oz) coconut milk
- 1 cup chicken or duck stock
- 1 tbsp fish sauce
- 1 tbsp brown sugar
- 1 red bell pepper, sliced
- 1 cup bamboo shoots, sliced
- 1/2 cup Thai basil leaves
- 2 tbsp vegetable oil

Instructions:

1. **Cook Duck:** Heat vegetable oil in a pan over medium-high heat. Add duck slices and cook until browned. Remove from pan and set aside.
2. **Make Curry Sauce:** In the same pan, add red curry paste and cook for 1-2 minutes until fragrant.
3. **Add Liquids:** Pour in coconut milk and stock, stirring to combine. Bring to a simmer.
4. **Add Vegetables:** Add bell pepper and bamboo shoots. Simmer until vegetables are tender.
5. **Finish:** Return duck to the pan, stir in fish sauce and brown sugar. Cook until heated through. Garnish with Thai basil before serving.

Japanese Tonkatsu

Ingredients:

- 4 pork loin chops
- Salt and pepper to taste
- 1/2 cup all-purpose flour
- 2 large eggs, beaten
- 1 cup panko breadcrumbs
- Vegetable oil for frying
- Tonkatsu sauce for serving

Instructions:

1. **Prepare Pork:** Season pork chops with salt and pepper.
2. **Bread Pork:** Dredge pork in flour, dip in beaten eggs, and coat with panko breadcrumbs.
3. **Fry Pork:** Heat vegetable oil in a skillet over medium-high heat. Fry pork until golden brown and cooked through, about 4-5 minutes per side.
4. **Serve:** Slice and serve with Tonkatsu sauce.

Korean Spicy Pork Belly

Ingredients:

- 1 lb pork belly, sliced
- 2 tbsp gochujang (Korean red chili paste)
- 2 tbsp soy sauce
- 1 tbsp sugar
- 1 tbsp sesame oil
- 4 cloves garlic, minced
- 1 tbsp ginger, minced
- 1 onion, sliced
- 2 green onions, chopped
- Sesame seeds for garnish

Instructions:

1. **Marinate Pork:** In a bowl, mix gochujang, soy sauce, sugar, sesame oil, garlic, and ginger. Add pork belly and marinate for at least 30 minutes.
2. **Cook Pork:** Heat a pan over medium-high heat. Add pork belly and onion. Cook until pork is browned and cooked through, about 5-7 minutes.
3. **Serve:** Garnish with green onions and sesame seeds. Serve with rice.

Vietnamese Bun Cha

Ingredients:

- 1 lb ground pork
- 2 tbsp fish sauce
- 2 tbsp sugar
- 2 cloves garlic, minced
- 1/4 cup chopped cilantro
- 1/4 cup chopped green onions
- 1/2 cup rice vinegar
- 2 tbsp sugar
- 1 cup water
- 1 cup cooked rice noodles
- Fresh herbs (mint, cilantro), lettuce, and pickled vegetables for serving

Instructions:

1. **Prepare Pork Patties:** Mix ground pork with fish sauce, sugar, garlic, cilantro, and green onions. Shape into small patties.
2. **Grill Patties:** Grill or pan-fry patties until cooked through, about 4-5 minutes per side.
3. **Make Sauce:** In a bowl, mix rice vinegar, sugar, and water. Stir until sugar is dissolved.
4. **Serve:** Serve patties with rice noodles, fresh herbs, lettuce, pickled vegetables, and dipping sauce.

Chinese Szechuan Eggplant

Ingredients:

- 1 lb eggplant, cut into bite-sized pieces
- 2 tbsp vegetable oil
- 2 cloves garlic, minced
- 1 tbsp ginger, minced
- 2 tbsp soy sauce
- 2 tbsp rice vinegar
- 1 tbsp Szechuan peppercorns
- 1 tbsp hoisin sauce
- 1 tbsp chili paste (optional)
- 1/4 cup water
- Chopped green onions for garnish

Instructions:

1. **Cook Eggplant:** Heat oil in a pan over medium-high heat. Add eggplant and cook until tender, about 5-7 minutes. Remove and set aside.
2. **Make Sauce:** In the same pan, add garlic, ginger, Szechuan peppercorns, soy sauce, rice vinegar, hoisin sauce, and chili paste. Stir and cook for 2 minutes.
3. **Combine:** Return eggplant to the pan and add water. Stir until eggplant is well coated and sauce is slightly thickened.
4. **Serve:** Garnish with chopped green onions. Serve with rice.

Thai Lemongrass Chicken

Ingredients:

- 1 lb chicken thighs, boneless and skinless
- 2 stalks lemongrass, minced
- 3 cloves garlic, minced
- 2 tbsp fish sauce
- 2 tbsp soy sauce
- 1 tbsp brown sugar
- 1 tbsp vegetable oil
- Fresh cilantro for garnish

Instructions:

1. **Marinate Chicken:** Mix lemongrass, garlic, fish sauce, soy sauce, and brown sugar. Marinate chicken for at least 30 minutes.
2. **Cook Chicken:** Heat oil in a pan over medium heat. Cook chicken until browned and cooked through, about 6-8 minutes per side.
3. **Serve:** Garnish with fresh cilantro. Serve with rice.

Japanese Okonomiyaki

Ingredients:

- 1 cup all-purpose flour
- 1/2 cup dashi stock
- 1 egg
- 1 cup shredded cabbage
- 1/2 cup sliced green onions
- 1/2 cup cooked bacon, chopped
- 2 tbsp vegetable oil
- Okonomiyaki sauce and bonito flakes for serving

Instructions:

1. **Make Batter:** In a bowl, whisk together flour, dashi stock, and egg. Stir in cabbage, green onions, and bacon.
2. **Cook Pancakes:** Heat oil in a pan over medium heat. Pour batter into the pan, forming a large pancake. Cook until golden brown on both sides, about 4-5 minutes per side.
3. **Serve:** Top with okonomiyaki sauce and bonito flakes.

Korean Steamed Egg

Ingredients:

- 4 large eggs
- 1 cup water
- 1/2 tsp salt
- 1/2 tsp sesame oil
- Chopped green onions for garnish

Instructions:

1. **Prepare Mixture:** In a bowl, whisk together eggs, water, and salt.
2. **Steam:** Pour mixture into a heatproof dish. Steam over simmering water for 10-15 minutes, or until set.
3. **Serve:** Drizzle with sesame oil and garnish with chopped green onions. Serve hot.

Vietnamese Egg Coffee

Ingredients:

- 2 large egg yolks
- 2 tbsp sweetened condensed milk
- 1/2 cup strong brewed Vietnamese coffee
- 1/4 cup milk
- 1/2 tsp vanilla extract (optional)

Instructions:

1. **Prepare Coffee:** Brew a strong cup of Vietnamese coffee.
2. **Make Egg Mixture:** In a bowl, whisk egg yolks with sweetened condensed milk until frothy and thick.
3. **Heat Milk:** Warm the milk in a saucepan or microwave until hot but not boiling.
4. **Combine:** Pour the brewed coffee into a cup. Gently spoon the egg mixture over the coffee.
5. **Serve:** Optionally, add a few drops of vanilla extract. Serve immediately, enjoying the creamy, frothy topping.

Chinese Peking Duck

Ingredients:

- 1 whole duck (about 5-6 lbs)
- 2 tbsp honey
- 2 tbsp soy sauce
- 1 tbsp rice vinegar
- 1 tbsp hoisin sauce
- 1 tbsp five-spice powder
- 1/2 tsp salt
- 1/2 tsp black pepper
- 1/2 cup water
- Pancakes, hoisin sauce, and sliced scallions for serving

Instructions:

1. **Prepare Duck:** Rinse the duck and pat dry. Remove excess fat from inside the cavity.
2. **Season Duck:** Rub the duck inside and out with salt, pepper, and five-spice powder.
3. **Glaze Duck:** Mix honey, soy sauce, rice vinegar, and hoisin sauce. Brush this mixture all over the duck.
4. **Roast Duck:** Place the duck on a rack over a roasting pan. Roast in a preheated oven at 375°F (190°C) for about 1.5 to 2 hours, basting occasionally with the remaining glaze.
5. **Crisp Skin:** Increase the oven temperature to 425°F (220°C) for the last 10-15 minutes to crisp the skin.
6. **Serve:** Let the duck rest before carving. Serve with pancakes, hoisin sauce, and sliced scallions.

www.ingramcontent.com/pod-product-compliance
Lightning Source LLC
LaVergne TN
LVHW061954070526
838199LV00060B/4116